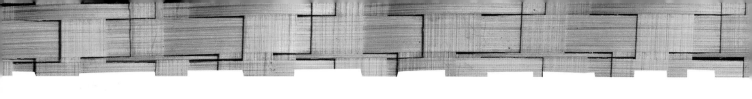

Picture credits:
l: Left, r: Right, t: Top, b: Bottom, c: Centre

Cover images: Front Cover: Misha Shiyanov/Shutterstock
Back Cover: ml: Vladimir Suponev/Istockphoto, mr: Eric Simard/Istockphoto, br: Melanie DeFazio/Shutterstock

Shutterstock:
6b: Johanna Goodyear, 7b: Misha Shiyanov, 8b: William Casey, 9t: Maria Dryfhout,
9b: Gleb Semenjuk, 13b: Jeff Thrower, 14m: Suponev Vladimir Mihajlovich, 15l: Antonio Jorge Nunes,
15m: Indigo Fish, 15r: Eric Isselée, 18b: April Turner, 19t: Mary Bingham,
20t: Johanna Goodyear, 21b, 21t: Simone van den Berg, 22b: Andrew Howe, 23: Alfred Wekelo,
24b: Sonya Etchison, Suponev Vladimir Mihajlovich, 26t: Simone van den Berg, Graeme Dawes,
27b: Tony Campbell, 28b: Aleksejs Kostins, 29b: Tatiana Popova, 30t: Tony Campbell,
31l: Eugene Bochkarev, 31r: Perrush, 32b: Jon Rasmussen, 33tr: Mikhail Olykainen,
34b: Stefan Glebowski, 35t: Lincoln Rogers, 37b: Tatiana Morozova, 38t: Piotr Przeszlo,
39t: Daniel Chadwick, 39b: Stephen Coburn, 41t: Alin Popescu, 41b: Pixshots,
42b: Alfred Wekelo, 43b: Dana Heinemann

Istockphoto:
7t: Andreea Manciu, 14t: Indigo Betta, 14b: Michael Chen, 16t: Missing35mm, 19b: Przemyslaw Rzeszutko,
29t: Jclegg, 40b: Denis Tabler, 42mr: Dimitry Romanchuck, 43t: Jallfree

Dreamstime.com:
12b: Ijansempoi, 13t: Bedo, 16b: Siberia, 17t, 17m, 17b: Andreystratilatov.com, 33tl: Kasiden,
33b: Raycan, 36t: Eei_tony

All illustrations made by Q2A Media.

American Edition Editor: Sean Kennelly

Caring for Cats and Kittens

CONTENTS

Introduction

Are you a cat lover? Are you planning to bring home a new kitty? That's a lovely idea. But you need to know a lot of things before you actually go and buy a furry companion for yourself.

Other Family Members

Check if your parents are equally happy about you bringing home a new cat or kitten. Not all people like pets at home. Also, some family members might prefer a different type of animal. Make sure you have the right kind of friendly atmosphere at home and that your cat or kitten will be treated lovingly as a pet and not a pest.

A family with their pet cat

Things You Need to Know

You should know about the behavior of cats and kittens: about different breeds and characteristics; about health and general care; about what they like and what they don't. You should also register your cat or kitten with a vet. You should have some idea about the charges and other expenses involved in keeping a pet. Consult your parents and make sure you can afford all the expenses. You also need to find the right places to buy a new cat or kitten.

Consult Your Friends

Some of your friends might have pets at home. Share their experiences and take advice from them. Make notes of important points you learn from them, and check with an expert if all the information is true. You may also talk to other people you trust.

Common Questions

If I buy a cat or kitten, do I always have to be around?

No, buying a cat or a kitten doesn't mean you give up going to school or the playground. You may even go on vacation. You just need to make the proper arrangements if you are going to be away. After all, your cat or kitten is your responsibility.

🐾 *You need to be a good friend to your cat or kitten*

Cat Breeds

There are many breeds of cat in the world.
Many of them are good natured, nice and adorable.

Siamese Cats

Siamese cats originate from Thailand, previously known as Siam. Now they are found in many houses in America and other countries. They have beautiful blue eyes and are very loving in nature. Siamese cats are very friendly and can mix well both with children and adults. They are intelligent animals and should become friendly with other pets in the house. These cats also require little grooming. Siamese cats are a calm breed but are known for their unique voice.

Persian Cats

It is believed that Persian cats were orginally found in Persia (modern day Iran). Now these cats can be found all across the globe. With their large expressive eyes, rounded ears, high nose, and chubby cheeks they are loving and affectionate animals. They mix well with other pets in the family. Hence, Persian's are a popular breed. They have very soft and long hair. Persian cats have a strong build and easily adapt to their environment. However, they require a lot of grooming and care. There are many types of Persian cats. The famous Himalayan cat is a well-known Persian breed.

Oriental cats make very good pets because they bond well with humans

Siamese cats have almond shaped eyes and a flat coat

8

Top Tips

In very humid and warm
weather conditions, you must
brush your cat or kitten
regularly. Shedding the excess
fur will help them to feel light,
comfortable and happy.

🐾 *Persian cats need regular
grooming to maintain
their long and dense fur*

Other Breeds

The Abyssinian breed is very graceful. With big
expressive eyes and a shiny coat, they look
very attractive. They can live for more than 20
years. Oriental breeds of cat are known for
their striking green eyes and colorful bodies.
Oriental cats have very long tails and soft,
silky hair. They are very playful cats and love
to make a lot of noise. They are usually very
active and love to be with their master.

Buying a Cat

You can buy your cats or kitten from one of several places. Once you have made up your mind to buy a cat or kitten, you may visit a breeder, a rescue shelter or a pet shop.

Breeders

Cat breeders will carefully plan and breed species to produce nice, fit and healthy cats and kittens. They take note of the health and temperament. Cat breeders not only sell their breeds, but sometimes use their choicest cats and kittens for public shows. But not all breeders are equally reliable. It is always better to buy your cat or kitten from a reputable breeder. It's a good idea to find a breeding club to help you identify the right breeder.

🐾 *Visit several breeders before you choose the cat or kitten you want to buy*

Rescue Shelters

Many cats and kittens each year are abandoned and left homeless. Rescue shelters take care of such cats and kittens and look after the sick or abandoned. Only after the cats and kittens are healthy again and have learned good manners are they sold. If you buy a cat or a kitten from a rescue shelter, you can be sure of its health and temperament. However, buying a cat and kitten from a rescue home may be a lengthy process. They will ask you to fill-in forms and will do a reference check to see if they are selling the cat or kitten to someone who can take good care of it.

🐾 *Rescue shelters are a good option because they take very good care of pets and will give you a nice and healthy cat or kitten.*

When you go to buy your cat or kitten from a pet shop, always ask about the breed and other details of the pet.

Common Questions

How do I find out about cat or kitten breeders in my town?

You can locate a good breeder though pet clubs. You can also look for advertisements in newspapers to locate breeders in your town. Always take an adult with you before you decide on buying your cat or kitten.

Pet Shops

Pet shops are another common place where you can get a cat or kitten. Cats and kittens in pet shops come either from private owners or from commercial cat and kitten farms. Unlike a reputable breeder, farms are usually less concerned about the health and temperament of the pets. Often there will also be less information about the background or breeding history of the cats and kittens available there.

Hello Kitty

When you bring a cat or kitten home for the first time they will need some time to adapt. But don't worry, they will gradually become familiar with the new environment, as well as the people and other pets.

This is Your Home

As the cat or kitten enters your home, take it around to make it familiar with every part of your house. Initially, your new pet might feel threatened. So, make sure you give your cat or kitten a space to hide when scared. It is best to confine it to a room for a few days. Spend a lot of time with your pet in that room.

You need to make your pet cat or kitten feel comfortable in its new surroundings.

Other Pets

It is best to think carefully before buying a cat or kitten. Consider the nature of the other pets you have at home as well as the cat or kitten you plan to buy. A lot depends on compatibility when there is more than one pet in a house. Quiet and serious cats or kittens may find it difficult to be around more active animals. While your new cat or kitten is confined to one room, try to gradually make them aware of the other pets' presence. With time, they should happily mix freely.

Your new cat or kitten may fight with other pets in the house before it gets familiar with them.

Top Tips

Always be around when you are letting your new cat or kitten and other pets interact for the first time.
Let this happen in an open space, so that if one of them attacks the other, the latter can easily escape.

Your new cat or kitten may take some time before it starts interacting with the other pets in the house.

Watch How They React

If the new pet starts fighting with existing pets, take your new pet back to its room. Keep it there for a few days and try the whole thing over. If the other pet is a bigger or more powerful animal like a dog, be very careful, because chances are that the dog might attack your cat or kitten. If the cat or kitten is in danger of being attacked and cannot escape, it might even attack you out of fear.

Much in a Name

Naming cats and kittens may not be as easy as you might think. Try to think of a name that is fun and distinctive.

Things to Consider

First check whether your cat or kitten is male or female. Look at its physical features. Larger cats or kittens might suit different names to smaller breeds. If the cat or kitten is soft and woolly you could perhaps name it Fluffy. Think of the cat or kitten's nature. A very active cat or kitten might be called Sparky. A sweet and good-natured one could be called Cuddles. Certain boy names will not be appropriate for female cats and, of course, certain female names will not suit boy cats.

Popular Cat Names

Max, Maggie, Buddy and Bailey are just a few of the most popular cat or kitten names. But why not try to be more creative with the name you give your cat or kitten. Look at their particular habits and characteristics for inspiration. Perhaps they make a particular noise or react in a certain way to something that makes you think of a distinctive name.

Cat Names and Categories

Some people might name their cat or kitten based on their breed, or their color. A name for white furry cats and kittens may not suit black ones. Lists of cat or kitten names based on these categories are available on several websites. However, if you look for too many names you might just find yourself more confused.

I wish they called me Hazard

They call me Nacho

Common Questions

How can I make sure that my cat or kitten really likes its name?

While deciding a name for your cat or kitten, call it by all the names you have shortlisted for it. Keep calling the cat or kitten by each of those names for a while and see if it reacts to any of them.

I would like to be called Cuddles

Don't Be Catty

If you want to see your cat or kitten happy, you should spend time alone with it. This will help develop a friendly bond. You should show your feelings and take good care of it. Don't be rude to it or scare it.

Make Friends

Stroke your cat or kitten often to make it feel special. This way it will know you and get used to you too. Initially, you may find it nervous or uncomfortable when you try to cuddle it. In that case stop until it calms down. You can play with its paws and rub its pads. Make the cat or kitten feel used to being touched slowly and soon it will be your best friend!

Play with your cat or kitten often. They will like your company

Since your cat or kitten has come to a new place, give it time to adjust

Understanding Body Language

Your cat or kitten may use its nose, eyes, touch, voice and even body language to communicate with you. It may try to tell you about its problems or ups and downs of mood. When it looks directly into your eyes, it means it trusts you. When it is happy, its eyes slant.

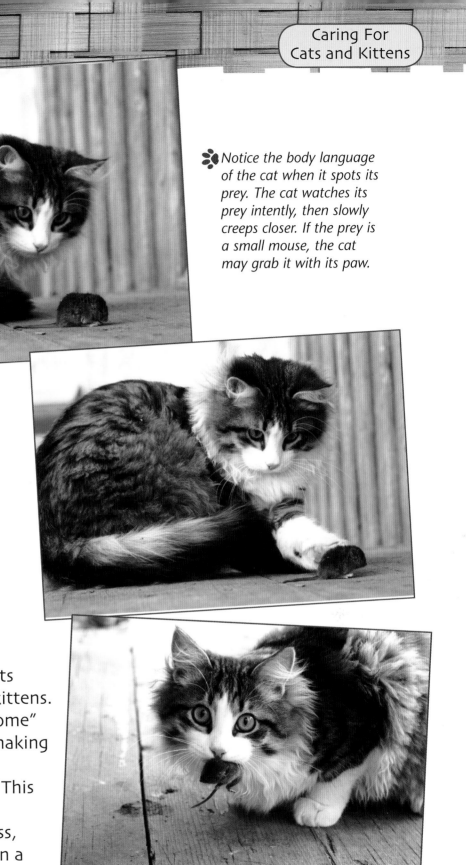

🐾 *Notice the body language
of the cat when it spots its
prey. The cat watches its
prey intently, then slowly
creeps closer. If the prey is
a small mouse, the cat
may grab it with its paw.*

Top Tips

If your cat or kitten
raises its tail high when
it sees you, it means it is
very happy!

Cat Speak

A cat or kitten often meows to its
owner like a mother cat to her kittens.
It may mean, "I'm glad you're home"
or "Feed me, now!" Instead of making
a sound your cat or kitten may
silently rub up against your leg. This
usually means they want some
attention, such as a stroke. A hiss,
spit or growl shows your pet is in a
serious mood. It is best to leave them
alone for a little while. A cat or kitten
usually purrs when it is content, but purring may
also mean it is trying to tell you something else.

Kitty Party

Cats and kittens are often fussy when it comes to food. They have strong likes and dislikes. To keep your cat or kitten healthy, you should know what they like to eat and what is good for their health.

Dry or Wet?

There are broadly two types of cat food available in the market — dry and wet. Dry food has very large amounts of carbohydrates. Too many carbohydrates can be harmful to your pet, so it needs a balance of both dry and wet food. Wet food in moderation is good for your cat or kitten. The proportion of protein in wet food is higher than that in dry food.

🐾 *Your cat or kitten should be given food to balance proteins and carbohydrates*

Common Questions

?

Can lack of water cause a cat or kitten to dehydrate?

Yes, reduced water intake causes dehydration, can cause kidney related diseases and, in the worse cases, death.

Meat versus Plants

Proteins found in dry cat food are mostly plant based. But your cat or kitten needs meat-based proteins to stay fit and healthy. This is found in wet food. When choosing your cat or kitten's wet food, make sure you choose a reliable provider. Check the label to be sure of the contents and pick wet food that shows a high meat content. Some wet food might come in jelly and some might come in gravy. Both contain healthy minerals and fats that your pet needs. They might, however, have a preference, so try both to see which they like more.

🐾 *Your cat or kitten can be given milk in small quantities as a special treat*

Water, Water

In the wild a cat or kitten's natural prey would contain about 75% water. You should ensure that your cat or kitten recieves this much water even when it eats cat food. Cats and kittens usually don't drink a lot of water as their food will provide most of what they need. However, it is still vital that you keep a fresh supply of clean water always available to your pet.

🐾 *Cats and kittens love to catch mice*

Taking Care

Regular combing of the fur coat of your cat or kitten will ensure that there are no lumps or mats of unwanted hair

You should regularly clean and groom your cat or kitten. This will help keep them hygienic, healthy and safe from diseases.

Combing

You should buy a special comb for your pet. Your cat or kitten's hair should be combed regularly. Choose a time when both you and your pet are in a relaxed mood. Your cat or kitten might become very restless when you start combing their hair. Begin by gently stroking, scratching and tickling the cat or kitten. You can start combing once you put it at ease. Your cat or kitten may have patches of matted hair. If you comb forcefully through such lumps of hair, you will hurt your pet, so be gentle.

Cleaning

Cats or kittens do not require bathing everyday. But sometimes they need to be given a wash. Wash your cat or kitten with lukewarm water. Never pour water directly on the head. Always use a cat shampoo while bathing your cat or kitten and be sure to wash out all the shampoo after cleaning it. Remove as much moisture as you can using a soft towel. Avoid using hair-dryers. Say nice things to your cat or kitten while cleaning. This will help your pet feel comfortable.

Nail Care

Your cat or kitten has what are known as retractable claws. These claws are very sharp and are always growing - much like your fingernails do. The cat or kitten uses these claws to help it grip when climbing and jumping. It will also use its claws when it hunts or, indeed, when it needs to defend itself. These sharp claws can be a nuisance in the home if your pet scratches your furniture. the best way to avoid this is to buy a scratching pole.

Top Tips

You should clean your cat or kitten's ears regularly. Ear mites often grow in their ears. This can be quite painful and even quite harmful for your pet unless cleaned properly.

CAT SHAMPOO

🐾 *Use cat shampoo to give your cat or kitten a clean and sparkling look*

🐾 *Your cat or kitten maintains their claws by scratching. Buy them a scratching pole to prevent them scratching your furniture*

Protecting Your Cat

Like most animals, cats and kittens are prone to several diseases, some of which can even be fatal. You should be watchful if your cat or kitten contracts any of those diseases and take immediate action.

🐾 *Your cat or kitten can lose weight and fall sick if it goes off its food*

🐾 *In case of a kidney disease, your cat or kitten should be fed food rich in Vitamin B*

Fussy Eaters

Some cats can be fussy eaters. This is thought to be due to the fact that they are unable to taste sugars. Unlike most animals, cats are able to voluntarily starve themselves if they are presented with a food they are not used to, or if they become bored of a food they are fed regularly. Although it is rare for this self-starving to lead to injury, you should be aware of your pet's intake of food and watch for rapid weight loss. If in doubt, take your cat or kitten to the vet as soon as possible.

Kidney Diseases

You should take your cat or kitten for a BUN (blood, urine, nitrogen concentration) test every year after it is six years old. A BUN tests whether your cat or kitten has kidney related problems. Symptoms include scratching, fatigue, thirst, and frequent urination. In case of a kidney disease, your cat or kitten should be fed meat proteins, lots of water and food with reduced sodium.

Constipation

Constipation among cats and kittens is common. Sometimes constipation may lead to obstipation, which can be very dangerous. During constipation it becomes difficult for your cat or kitten to pass feces. Obstipation is a state when your cat or kitten cannot pass feces at all. This is a serious problem and needs to be checked by a vet. You should regularly monitor your cat or kitten's litter tray to make sure they are passing solid waste regularly.

You should consult a vet if your cat or kitten develops any health problems

Common Questions

Should I add laxatives and cathartic drugs to my cat or kitten's food during constipation?

You may use laxatives, which are usually milder. But before adding cathartic drugs it is better you consult a vet. Cathartic drugs are very strong and can lead to diarrhea.

Etikitty

Everyone wants well-behaved cats and kittens, who won't be a menace for the household. Cats and kittens, if not trained properly, can cause damage to furniture, carpets and even clothes.

Reward Them

While training your cat or kitten, don't try to force them or scold them if they do something wrong. Reward them when they do as you want. They should get the feeling that it is convenient and better to be well behaved rather than unruly. Cats or kittens are not expected to learn by mere instructions, but slowly acquire good habits by practice followed by rewards.

You should reward your cat or kitten when it listens to your instructions and is well behaved

You can buy different colored litter boxes for your cat or kitten

Litter Training

Litter training is very important if you don't want your cat or kitten to spoil your home. You should follow a fixed routine when feeding your cat or kitten. This will ensure that your pet will relieve itself at more or less a fixed time. Stand near the litter box and call your pet from wherever it is. Do something to attract the cat or kitten towards the litter box (such as shaking a toy or some dry food). Make sure you have a layer of fresh cat litter in the tray because your cat or kitten's instinct is to scratch loose material over its feces. Reward your pet when it uses the litter tray correctly.

Litter Tray Hygiene

Just as you keep the bathroom and toilet clean in your home, so you should keep your cat or kitten's litter tray clean. But, don't worry, you don't have to change the litter every day! You should remove feces from the litter with a scoop every day or so. Once a week, throw away the litter and thoroughly clean the tray with soap and water. Allow the tray to dry before placing fresh litter back in the tray.

Thoroughly clean out your cat or kitten's litter tray about once a week

Top Tips

When cleaning out your cat or kitten's litter tray you might want to wear protective gloves. Remember your own hygiene is most important. Sterilize the area where you have washed the litter tray out and thoroughly wash your hands once you have finished.

You could buy a toy mouse for your cat or kitten to chase at home

Keeping Fit

Regular exercise keeps cats and kittens fit and healthy. Unlike a dog, which requires regular walks in order to stay fit, cats are very good at exercising themselves. However, you may need to buy a few toys to keep your cat or kitten active.

Cat in a Box

You can start with a ball or a crumpled piece of paper. Throw it on the floor and let your cat or kitten jump on it. You can also use a box and keep the ball inside it. Your cat or kitten will be curious to get in and see what is inside. Keep repeating this game to provide some fun both for you and your cat or kitten. You could even use a battery-operated mouse instead of a ball of paper. Your pet cat or kitten will have a lovely time trying to catch it.

Catch it if you Can

You could arrange something for your cat or kitten to chase around, thus building up its muscles as well as it being happily active. Your cat or kitten is predatory by nature and will love this chasing game. You can use balls, teaser wands or even mouse toys for this. You can also arrange something for the cat or kitten to climb, placing an object on top of it. There are many types of cat toys available in shops. Be creative and enjoy the moments you spend playing with your cat or kitten.

Love of Heights

Some cats and kittens will show a love of high (and sometimes dangerous) places, such as the edges of rooftops. Cats have excellent balance and are also capable of falling significant distances without hurting themselves. However, especially with younger kittens, it might be wise to block-off more dangerous heights. Be warned though: cats are excellent climbers and, if they really want to get somewhere, they'll usually find a way!

You should keep an eye on your cat or kitten to try to prevent them from hurting themselves

Playing with balls of wool can be fun for your cat or kitten

Common Questions

**What is catnip?
Do all cats respond to it?**

Catnip is a herb. Most cats and kittens become hyperactive if exposed to catnip. However, kittens below three months do not respond to it. Most (but not all) grown up cats respond to catnip.

Cat Gifts

Cats and kittens, like us, love gifts. It makes them happy when you buy them a gift on their birthday. There could be many other occasions when you treat your pet, and there are endless options of gifts to choose from.

Cat Bedding

You could buy your cat or kitten a warm and fancy angora kennel or a warm bed. This will definitely make your pet happy. There are many types of cosy cat beds available in shops. You can even buy them over the internet. You could buy your little kitty a round or oval cat bed. There are very soft and colorful beds for cats or kittens as well as more durable hardy ones. Along with a bed you could also bring home some fancy duvet or blanket for your cat or kitten, which they will love.

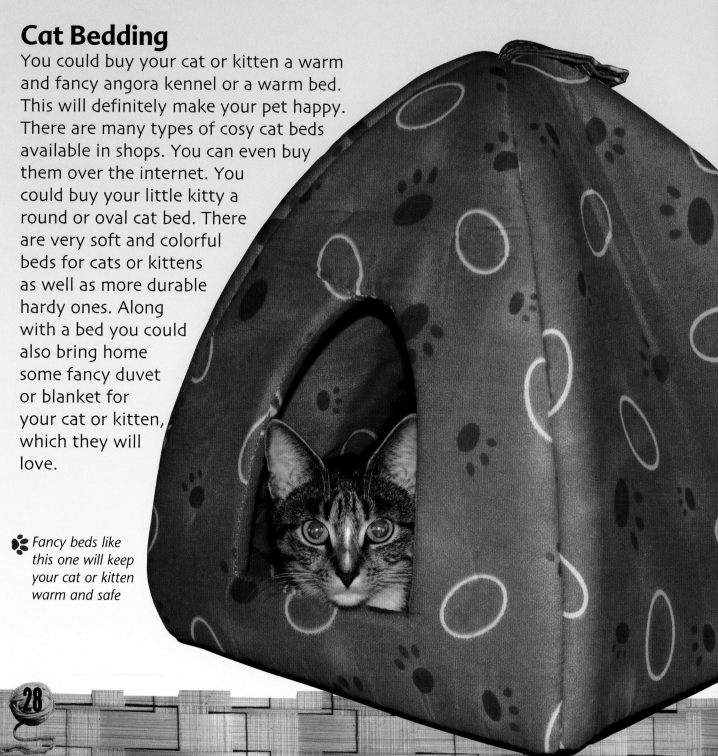

Fancy beds like this one will keep your cat or kitten warm and safe

Accessories

You might like to buy your cat or kitten a beautiful collar in order to make them look smart. Make sure any collar or harness is comfortable to wear. Do not use cat collars until your kitten is six months old. Measure your cat or kitten's neck before buying a collar so that it fits perfectly. It is also a good idea to attach a name tag with your contact details to the collar so that, if your pet becomes lost, you are easily contactable.

Measure the size of the collar before you buy one for your cat or kitten

Eating Aides

You could buy your cat or kitten a bowl or feeder on its birthday. Feeders and bowls come in all kinds of shapes and designs. Find one your cat or kitten seems most comfortable with using. Drinking fountains are also available for cats and kittens. You could even opt for a cat-feeding mat. Your cat or kitten will love eating on those and it will also help to keep your floor clean.

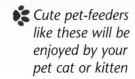

Cute pet-feeders like these will be enjoyed by your pet cat or kitten

Beat the Heat

Your cat or kitten will need special care during summer, as heat and sun can be really dangerous.

Heat Stroke

Heat stroke is a potentially fatal condition, where the body organs cannot function due to exposure to heat. A cat or kitten's usual body temperature ranges from 100.5-102.5 Fahrenheit (38-39.1 Celsius). Make sure your cat or kitten has easy access to shade indoors during hot summer months. Cats and kittens are usually very good at keeping out of the heat themselves, but if you find your cat or kitten panting or dizzy, very weak, its gums turning dark red or very pale, or bleeding from the nose, it could be signs of a severe heat stroke.

Your cat or kitten should have easy access to shade and water during hot summer months

Dehydration

Heat stroke can lead to severe dehydration. Apart from sun stroke there could be several reasons for dehydration - like vomiting and diarrhea, loss of appetite and reduced water intake, fever or blood loss. Ensure that your pet cat or kitten has easy access to a regularly-refreshed supply of water. Remember that your cat or kitten gets most of their liquid intake from food, so make sure they are fed properly too.

Your cat or kitten needs extra care and attention when it falls ill

Some General Measures

Put ice cubes in your cat or kitten's water bowl. Wrap ice in a towel and place it next to your cat or kitten. You could put towels in the freezer and then place them near the cat or kitten's bed for it to lie on whenever it is hot. If you have any fans you could angle them towards the ground so that your cat or kitten feels the benefit. Remember, older and overweight cats, as well as some breeds like Persians and Exotics, are more prone to heat stroke than other cats.

Give your cat or kitten cold water to drink to help avoid heat stroke

Common Questions

Should I apply sunscreen to my cat or kitten's body on hot summer days?

Yes, you can apply sunscreen to your cat or kitten's nose and ears when it is very hot, to prevent your cat or kitten from getting sunburnt.

Wintry Nights

Like in summer, cats and kittens also need special care in winter. During winter months, cats and kittens should be kept warm. Providing a proper shelter for your cat or kitten is just the beginning of your responsibilities.

Keep it Warm

The room you have allotted to your cat or kitten to stay in should be insulated and properly heated. Your cat or kitten should not be left to sleep on the floor. Provide it with a thick and warm bed, as well as duvets and blankets to keep the cold away. Cats or kittens should also eat more in winter. This will add more calories, which in turn will help keep the body warm. If the temperature drops alarmingly during this season, do not let your cat or kitten outside. Keep it indoors so that it can be warm. If you do let your pet outside, make sure they have easy access in and out of the house so that they can come in easily when they are cold.

Let your cat or kitten play indoors during the winter months to keep warm and safe

Frostbite

If your cat or kitten spends too long outside when it is freezing, it may risk getting frostbite. You should be careful to remove any ice, snow or mud from your cat or kitten's feet as soon as it comes back. If it is frostbitten you will notice that your pet's skin has turned reddish, gray or white and the skin may also be scaly or peel off. Take your cat or kitten to the vet if you spot any of these symptoms.

Frostbite will cause the skin of your cat or kitten to peel off and become extremely painful

Top Tips

Whenever you suspect frostbite, apply a warm and moist towel on the frostbitten areas before you call on your vet. This stops things becoming worse.

You could dress up your cat or kitten during festive seasons

Holiday Food

Winter is a time when you love to party and eat lots of good food. This is the time for Halloween and Christmas. But it's important to remember that sweets, turkey, pork or other human food are not good for your cat or kitten. Do not change their regular diet in winter, but you can increase the amount of food they get. Especially at Christmas, make sure that small bones, as well as small decorations (or anything else that could get caught in your cat or kitten's throat), is kept out of reach.

Travelling with a Cat

Many people think that pet cats and kittens can be an inconvenience while you are vacationing away from home. However, travelling with them can be real fun - as long as you have planned the trip well and taken all precautions.

Before Setting Out

Before you set out on your journey you should consult your vet. Check your cat or kitten's health and the weather of the place where you are going. Make sure that where you are going to stay allows pets. Take your cat or kitten out on short local drives before actually setting out on a trip. You should attach an identity tag on your cat or kitten and also leave your itinerary with your vet.

Ensure that your cat or kitten is fit and healthy before you take it with you on a trip

About to Leave

When you are leaving for a long journey with your cat or kitten, make sure you carry plenty of food and water for it. Place your cat or kitten in a carrier and never let it out while you are driving. Cats or kittens usually feel uncomfortable on such occasions and behave oddly. They may cry aloud and try to get out of the carrier. Don't worry if that happens. Do not let the cat or kitten out of the carrier however much it may cry, as it might injure itself if the car brakes suddenly.

Common Questions

Can I put my cat or kitten on sedatives when setting out on long journeys?

Not always: sedatives do help at times, but a lot depends on the cat or kitten's health and nature. Always consult your vet on this.

🐾 Carriers not only stop your pet from creating a nuisance but also prevent other animals from attacking it

🐾 Carriers like these are well ventilated and are used to carry pets while travelling long distances. The arrows in the illustration show how air is circulated through the carrier

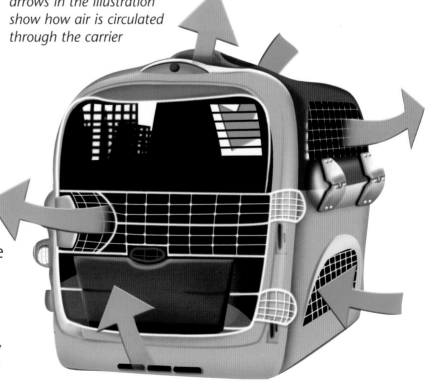

Traveling by Air

Most airlines do not allow cats or kittens to travel with the owner. There are special places in the airplane for pet cats and kittens. Some smaller airlines do not have the license to carry animals. If you are flying, always check with your particular airline first. Remember, if you are traveling to another country, you must check that you have all the necessary paperwork.

Leaving Alone

Cats are quite independent animals and it is possible to leave them on their own for 2-3 days at a time. It is recommended, however, that you don't leave kittens for more than a day.

🐾 *Be careful not to leave string or rope around when you are not there as it might be dangerous for your pet*

Make Your House Cat Proof

Before leaving your cat or kitten alone in your house, make sure you do not leave any expensive articles strewn on the floor, or in any area which can be easily reached. Also make sure that there is nothing left around the house that your pet might get entangled in. You should also be careful about sharp and pointed objects in the house. Any poison or medicines should also be kept out of reach.

Keeping Busy

Your cat or kitten needs something to play with when you are not around. Keep paper bags or cardboard boxes, which cats or kittens love to play with. Leave a tennis ball on the floor and scratching posts so that your cat or kitten does not end up scratching the furniture. Your pet should then be happy to entertain itself while you are away.

Pet feeders supply food at fixed intervals for your pet

Pet Feeder

While away, you have to ensure that there is enough food and water for your pet cat or kitten. Both dry and wet food can rot if left open for long hours. To avoid this you can use automatic pet feeders and waterers with timers, which will provide food and water at fixed times. You can use pet feeders even when you are home. This takes away much of your worries about feeding your cat or kitten at the right time.

Paper bags are a good way of keeping your pet cat or kitten entertained when you are away

Top Tips

Make sure your cat or kitten can get to their food, water and litter tray, their toys, and also their favorite place to sleep while you are away. Close the doors to rooms that they don't normally go in.

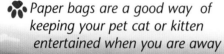

Watch Out!

Be careful when your beloved little kitty roams about in your house. Many articles in your house could appear completely harmless to you, but may pose a real threat to your cat or kitten.

Be careful to never leave your pet cat or kitten unattended near anything hot or burning in the house

Fire and Electricity

Your cat or kitten can be easily attracted towards the bright flames of your fireplace. Burning candles, left unattended, may be dangerous too. Be careful when you have anything burning in the house. Wires and appliances should be kept out of your pet's reach. Never leave a hot iron unattended when your cat or kitten is around.

Chocolates are Dangerous!

Chocolate, candy and alcohol can be very harmful for your pet cat or kitten. Medicines, antifreeze and insecticides or other poisons could also prove fatal to them. They should not have access to any of these. Cats and kittens might like the taste of chocolate but you must not let them have it. Chicken bones can lead to choking and should be kept away. Keep away other small objects that could be easily swallowed by your cat or kitten. There are also some types of plant that you shouldn't keep in the same house as a cat or kitten.

🐾 *Chocolate and candy can be extremely harmful for your pet cat or kitten*

🐾 *High baby cots will help keep your cat or kitten away from a baby at home*

Common Questions

Can the medicines we take when we are sick help our cats or kittens?

Never try medicines for humans on your cat or kitten. Always consult a vet when your pet is sick.

Keep Babies Away!

If you have a young child at home, you need to be very careful. Cats or kittens have a tendency to curl up to the bodies of babies as they find them warm and very comfortable. This is potentially very dangerous. Always keep your pet cat or kitten away from babies. A cat net, that protect babies from such mishaps, is strongly recommended.

Vaccination and Vet

Cats and kittens, like humans, need vaccines to stay healthy. Vaccines help cats and kittens fight germs and diseases. Always consult a vet and follow their advice and schedule for maintaining the health of your beloved new kitty.

Some Common Vaccines

The Rabies Virus Vaccine, Feline Herpesvirus Vaccine, Feline Leukemia Virus Vaccine, Chlamydia and Ringworm Vaccine: these are just a few common vaccines that vets may prescribe for pet cats and kittens. Each vaccine protects against a particular virus. Many vaccines are repeated every year; other vaccines need to be repeated after three years. It is not only kittens that need vaccinating, but fully-grown cats also.

🐾 *Consult your vet for all the vaccines needed for your cat or kitten*

Vaccination Side Effects

Vaccinating your cat or kitten can cause side effects. The reactions could be mild or very serious. In case of mild reactions your pet might catch a fever, sneeze and lose its appetite for a few days. There might be small swellings under the skin, which lasts for a few days. If any of these symptoms lasts for an unusually long time you should return to your vet for advice.

Top Tips

A vaccine for ringworm has come out that is available in certain parts of the world. Check with your vet if the vaccine is available in your country. This may free your pet from worm related troubles.

Your cat or kitten may eat grass when it does not feel well

 *Take your cat or kitten to the vet if you spot any unusual symptoms*

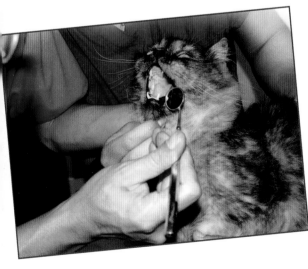

Things May Get Serious

Serious allergies to vaccination are potentially fatal to your cat or kitten, but serious reactions are rare. In such cases, your cat or kitten may react immediately, or the reaction may occur after some time. Sometimes, tumors or lumps may develop on the area of the skin where the vet has administered the vaccine. Tumors may not surface right away, but may take several weeks or months to emerge. If you have any concerns you should consult with your vet. They will do everything possible to protect the health of your animal.

First-Aid

Your pets may have accidents and you should keep a first-aid box handy for your cat or kitten just in case.

You should follow an agreed schedule when taking your cat or kitten to the vet

Eye Drops and Ear Drops

Your first-aid kit should contain eye drops and ear drops. Ear drops should be used to clean your pet cat or kitten's ears regularly. You could also use olive oil or almond oil as ear drops for your pets. In case you have run out of eye drops and you need some urgently, you can make some saline solution at home. Boil some water, then dissolve a little salt in it, before cooling it. This is a good remedy for times of emergency and can ease your pet cat or kitten's distress.

EYE DROPS

A vet checks the health of a cat's eyes

Antiseptic

You should always keep good antiseptic solution or cream. Some creams contain phenol and cresol which are harmful to cats and kittens, and should be avoided. You need to check the chemicals used in the antiseptic. Consult your vet about the right type of antiseptic for your kitty.

ANTISEPTIC CREAM
For animal use only

🐾 *Always keep a tube of antiseptic at home for minor accidents*

Other First-Aid Items

You should keep some fur-ball remedy, blunt-ended scissors, tweezers, and syringes. Syringes are not only needed to inject medicine, but also for liquid feeding. A thermometer, petroleum jelly and some plain kaolin mixture are also advised. Kaolin mixtures are used in the case of minor stomach problems. Do not forget to keep gauze, bandages and some cotton balls.

Common Questions

How do I restrain my cat or kitten when they are injured and in pain?

If your cat or kitten is in pain they may scratch or bite you if you try to apply first-aid.

Carefully hold them by the back of the neck and then press them down. You may also wrap them in a blanket to prevent them further injuring themselves by struggling.

First Aid Tape

Antiseptic solution

Gauze

Elastic Bandage

Cotton Balls

Absorbent Cotton
U.S.P Sterile
NET WT. 1/2 OZ (14.175 GRAMS)

🐾 *Prepare a small first-aid kit and always keep it in a place where you can reach it easily*

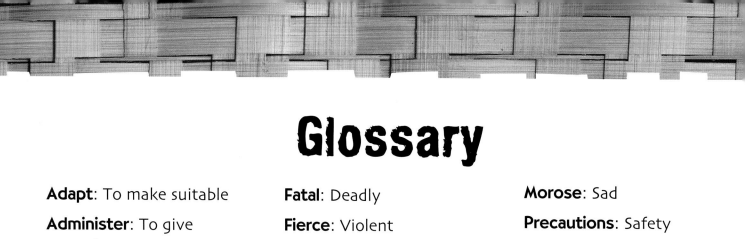

Glossary

Adapt: To make suitable

Administer: To give or apply

Aggressive: Angry and violent

Anesthesia: A drug given to make a body part numb

Antiseptic: Substance applied to reduce chance of infection

Appetite: Desire to eat

Breed: Particular species

Communicate: Share information

Convenient: Easy

Dehydration: Loss of water

Ear mites: Tiny organisms that live in the ears of animals

Entangled: Wrapped in

Fatal: Deadly

Fierce: Violent

Frostbite: Injury from exposure to freezing temperatures

Hygienic: Free from germs and diseases

Hyperactive: Excessively active

Initially: In the beginning

Itinerary: Plan of action

Laxatives: Medicine that aids in bowel movement

Menace: Trouble

Mishap: Accident

Morose: Sad

Precautions: Safety measures

Predatory: Living by feeding on other animals

Prey: Animals that are hunted

Purr: Soft call of the cat

Saline: Sterile saltwater mixture

Strewn: Scattered

Suffocation: Choking

Symptoms: Signs

Threatened: Feeling unsafe

Unruly: Badly behaved

Index